Finding the On-Ramp to Your Spiritual Path

Finding the On-Ramp to Your Spiritual Path

A ROAD MAP TO JOY AND REJUVENATION

JAN PHILLIPS

QUEST BOOKS

Theosophical Publishing House
Wheaton, Illinois • Chennai, India

Quest Books
Theosophical Publishing House
PO Box 270
Wheaton, IL 60187-0270

www.questbooks.net

Cover design by Drew Stevens

Library of Congress Cataloging-in-Publication Data

Phillips, Jan.
    Finding the on-ramp to your spiritual path: a road map to joy and rejuvenation / Jan Phillips.
        pages   cm.
ISBN 978-0-8356-0917-3
1. Spiritual life.   I. Title.
BL624.P525 2013
204'.4—dc23   2012049752

        5   4   3   2   1   *   13   14   15   16   17   18

Printed in the United States of America

TABLE OF CONTENTS

Introduction

My own journey has led me around the world, into the homes and lives of hundreds of people on the path to whom I feel profoundly connected. We come from all backgrounds, with roots in any number of religious traditions, but it is not these traditions that unify us. It is the commonness of our spiritual quest that brings us together—our steadfast, daily, joyful commitment to peace, enlightenment, compassion, and contact with the Divine that fuels and sustains us.

Each of us acknowledges that we are on a spiritual path, but none of us are on the same path. Some of us attend church; most of us celebrate our faith in our own sacred spaces—some with others, some alone. We are committed to deepening our relationships with people, making time for solitude and prayer, doing work that is consistent with our nature, contributing time and energy to community organizations, participating in events and rituals that foster self-awareness and self-expression. There is no mystique to the spiritual path. No initiation to undergo nor dues to pay. It is simply a journey of awareness through the landscape of one's life.

To be on a spiritual path means to live mindfully, paying attention to the signs along the road and being conscious of our body—the vehicle we are traveling in—and of the needs and safety of others on the journey.

To be on a spiritual path means to look inward as often as outward, knowing that the externals of our lives are reflections of our thoughts and words, manifestations of that which we are imagining and energizing into being with the fuel of our passion.

To be on a spiritual path means to use the rearview mirror to be sure that the path behind is clear of debris and that we do not obstruct another's journey with clutter of our own. It means making peace with our past, knowing our future contains it, and summoning the courage it takes to acknowledge, forgive, and release whatever we have clung to that impedes our movement.

To be on a spiritual path is to take responsibility for creating our own creed, based on our commitments, and to respect the rights of others to do the same. It also means to reflect anew on what beliefs we've inherited to be sure they are compatible with our wisdom and compassion.

To be on a spiritual path is to embrace the mystical paradox that while we are singular, physical beings on this journey, we are also profoundly connected to one another, animated and sustained by the same vast Spirit that abides in the star, the petal of an iris, the howl of the wolf.

To be on a spiritual path is to live with the awareness that your terror is mine, my hunger is yours, our longings are common. It is to remember that every breathing creature and plant is being breathed by the Cosmos at Large.

To be on a spiritual path, it is necessary to forgive yourself for wrong turns, for failing to yield, for driving under the influence of others. These are minor and forgivable infractions. The more important rules of this road are to be attentive, to notice when you stray, and to get back on the path as soon as possible.

We could all use a road map for the journey inward, a guide away from the crowded thoroughfare to the quiet path of our own true calling; a reminder that it is not the destination, but the journey, that is important. The fourteenth-century Italian saint Catherine of Siena once wrote, "All the way to heaven *is* heaven." Perhaps this is roadmap enough—this one stark line enough to keep us walking, reminding us that the wind we feel on the back of our necks is nothing less than the breath of God.

Preparing for the Journey

If you're new to the concept of a spiritual path, you probably have some questions like, What is it, anyway? Who else is on it? Where does it lead? Can I get lost? How much time does it take? Shall I wait until the kids are grown before I get on it? How much does it cost?

For starters, you are already on a path, just like everyone else. We are born. We have a journey called our life. Then we die. Those people who decide to focus on the inner journey, the path of the heart, are those who are on the spiritual path. They are people attempting to live fully in the present moment, aware that it's there and only there that one finds joy, peace, and communion.

They are not forfeiting today for some future bliss but living every moment as consciously as possible. They are artists who wake up every day to a fresh canvas of time, creating their days from their deepest desires. They are not the ones with all the answers but the ones with all the questions, reveling in the unraveling of life's unfolding mysteries.

As to where the path leads, it leads us to our bliss, and that is something that's unique to each of us. Bliss, to me, may be living in the woods or farming the land; to another, it may be creating a business, working for justice, making music, writing poetry, or raising children. Living in a culture bent on profit, it's hard to keep our ground and remember what we are here for, but we're all here for a purpose, and to live in bliss is to be true to that calling, that inner voice that guides us as we make our way home.

And, yes, you can get lost if you don't stay tuned to your inner voice. You can get lost if you look to others to tell you the way, if you follow the crowd for its safety of numbers, if you defer to another's authority without trusting your instincts. On the path of the heart, it is you who must choose when to turn and where, what to do and how. And those directions are always accessible when you pause and ponder, ask and listen. You will always know the next step when you let love and joy be your guide.

As for time, this is a journey that takes a lifetime. But remember, the spiritual path is the path of bliss. Why would you want it to be over soon? Every step is a step toward the light, taking you deeper and deeper into the radiance of the divine, which belongs to you intimately and infinitely. A perpetual state of enlightenment is unattainable. It is moments of enlightenment we're after, and they're strewn like jewels on the spiritual path. They shine into the darkest night, lighting our way through each unknown passage—a memory here, a tender touch there, a glimpse into the heartbreaking beauty of a child's face, a moment with another that illumines our oneness. These experiences do not go unnoticed by spiritual pilgrims. They fuel them, fortify them, anchor them to the real, and give them wings.

Shall you embark now on this path of the heart? Now, when your life is so full, when your children are tugging at your clothes, your loved ones calling from afar, the demands on your time more weighty than ever? Only if the voice within calls you to the path. Only if you are ready to choose freedom, to commit to living passionately and compassionately, to create with your own hands the circumstances of your life. Only if you are ready to abandon mediocrity and negativity, old voices, old certainties, old doubts. Only if you are brave enough to let go of the known and enter into the grandest of mysteries—the mystery of your Oneness with All Creation.

Do not set foot on this path if you are not prepared to pay the toll—the daily, demanding surrender of your fear. Do not come along if you are not willing to let go of your illusions, to give up your concepts for an experience of the Real. This journey goes deep into the darkness toward the Light beneath it. There are trails to places you have never been, sights along the way you have never seen—and unimaginable excursions into bliss, intimacy, and communion with others and the Divine within. Is the spiritual path for you? That is something only you can decide. If you are ready for the trip of a lifetime, come along.

Stop

Since the spiritual path is a path of mindfulness, the first step requires that you come to a complete stop, catch your breath, and be aware that wherever you are right now is the perfect place for you to be. All the choices you have made in your life have brought you here, and they deserve to be honored. Or as the Sufi mystic Hafiz would say, "The place where you are right now, God circled on a map for you."

So give yourself credit. Stop judging yourself. Stop being critical. Stop thinking negative thoughts. You have chosen the path of enlightenment, and that path is illumined from the inside out—*as we believe, so it becomes.*

The journey on which you are about to embark is a pilgrimage inward, and the destination is awareness. This is a guidebook for the joyful adventure of finding yourself; for once we know who we are, where we are, where we want to go, all heaven breaks loose with the possibility of fulfillment. Once you become mindful of your thoughts, your words, and your desires, you tune in also to the great power they hold; you tap your own potential to use them to create the kind of life you came here to experience. The more mindful you become, the more you will experience your creativity, and the more you will understand how it works. You will begin to feel in your flesh and bones the very inflow of the Creative Force that is collaborating with you at every moment.

The difference between people who are on the spiritual path and those who are not is a matter of consciousness. To be on the path means that you are living in the state of awareness. You are conscious of what you are doing and why you are doing it. You are conscious that you may not always have a choice about what happens to you, but you do have a choice about how you respond to it. And this is where you begin to experience your own life as something you are actually creating, because every move you make along the way is your own choice, your own creation.

A few years ago, I veered off the path and found myself in a stressful frenzy. I had begun graduate school thinking it would provide a scintillating, engaging environment. I imagined myself in Socrates's circle and found myself instead surrounded by students half my age concerned more with spring breaks in Cancun than anything else. I was disenchanted with the whole experience, found fault with everything and everyone, and worked my way into a mental and spiritual morass.

Totally out of balance, I called up my spiritual mentor, Paula, and informed her I was quitting school.

She listened to my outburst of negativity, then asked three questions: Are you eating and drinking moderately? Do you have a physical regimen for your body? Do you have a spiritual practice? I couldn't answer yes to any of them, and she said, "Jan, no wonder your life's a mess. You don't have any balance in it. Nothing can possibly work out for you if you don't take care of those three areas." She suggested I make some changes in my life, work on balance, and wait a few weeks to see how I felt about quitting school. "Call me before you do anything drastic," she said.

That morning I made a commitment to beginning each day with twenty minutes of silence before I got out of bed. That would be my spiritual practice. No newspapers. No books or TV or phone calls. I lit a candle and focused on my breath for twenty minutes. I bought a bicycle and started riding it to school instead of driving. I threw out the junk food

I had all over the house and started eating and drinking mindfully. They were not big changes, but they did require attention and vigilance. I shifted from automatic pilot to manual control for twenty-one days.

After three weeks I called Paula. "You are *not* going to believe what happened. Everyone on campus has changed dramatically!" I announced, full of joy and hopefulness. And she laughed right along with me, knowing that all the change I referred to had happened deep down inside me. I had stopped blaming people for not living up to my expectations, because I was no longer disgruntled. I was feeling good about myself and didn't have to blame anyone for my life being all wrong. I was eating well, drinking moderately, exercising daily, and staying true to my twenty minutes of silence a day. I had started down a spiritual path, and the journey felt adventurous and liberating.

You don't need to subscribe to religious dogma to be spiritual. Spirituality is not about creeds, saintly behavior, martyrdom, or selflessness. It is not about aspiring to be what we are not. It is about being everything we *are* with the greatest courage we can muster. It is about realizing—making real—our very selves. Meister Eckhart, a German mystic, writes that "when the soul wants to have an experience of something, she throws an image of that experience ahead of her and then enters into her own image." Being on the spiritual path is doing just that: envisioning what we want, then setting out with intention, desire, and diligence to get there. Whether or not we're "religious" or belong to a church has very little to do with it.

My uncle once said to me, "I'm not spiritual. I can't pray anymore." When I asked why, he said, "I forgot the words." He had confused spirituality with religion, thinking it had something to do with what he had once learned and had now forgotten. And come hunting season every fall, he would go to the hunting camp with his brothers, strike out on his own with his gun in hand, find a tree to sit under, and be alone with his thoughts. "I never fire a shot," he said. "I'm just waiting for a deer to come so that I can enjoy its wildness. It's the place I go to feel connected with nature. That's really my religion, but don't you dare tell anyone."

My uncle never thought of himself as being on a spiritual path. He didn't come to it with that kind of consciousness, and yet he knew where to go when he wanted to connect with the inner world. Hunting season was his stop sign in life. It was his chance to turn his back on the chaos of life and trudge into the woods, where he found his balance and bliss in communion with the wild.

Each of us must determine for ourselves what it takes to keep us balanced. This is the greatest gift we can give to ourselves, and therefore to our loved ones, for if we do not love ourselves lavishly, we cannot love others lavishly. And that is really what we are here for—to be a great light for others, to heal them with our touch and our deep listening, to mirror back to them their own majesty and magnitude.

So when you come to a stop sign on the road, let it be a reminder. Stop judging yourself. Start loving yourself. Think *balance* as you come to your complete stop, and after you look to the right and the left, look inward as well, to be sure you have what you need to stay steady on the path.

Lane Ends

I came to the end of a lane once, and it was terrifying. It was my first month in the convent and our first day of Theology 101. The tall, bulky Jesuit priest burst through the doorway, heaved his books on the desk, and turned to the thirty postulants before him saying, "All right, so you're going to dedicate your lives to God. Let's hear something about your relationship with this great love of your life."

This was easy, I thought. We had all been educated in Catholic schools and had memorized the Baltimore catechism. One by one, my classmates raised their hands, stood up, and repeated the answers we had been repeating all our lives.

"God made me to show his goodness and to share his life in everlasting happiness," said the first sister.

"That's the best you can do?" the priest replied.

"Yes, Father."

"Sit down!"

The next postulant took a shot. "God is the Father and the first person of the Holy Trinity."

"That's it?" he said.

"Yes, Father."

"Sit down!"

A third postulant met with the same disdain; then the room was quiet. What was he doing? I couldn't imagine what was wrong. The answers everyone was giving were perfect, and still he dismissed them and asked for more.

"This is the best you can do?" he shouted, his arms flailing heavenward. "You call this God of yours believable? None of you have said one thing I can believe in. This is nonsense you're uttering. What about your *relationship* with this God of yours?" A wave of anxiety rushed through me. I wanted to cry. Who was this terrible man and why was he doing this? Here we had offered up all we knew of God and he was taking a hammer to our cherished beliefs, shattering what we had clung to all our lives. It was devastating.

None of our beliefs stood up to his questions. Not one of us could defend our faith, for we had never learned the answers to the questions he was asking. We had learned *what* to think, but not *how* to think, and his questions ran deeper than any of our thoughts.

I sat frozen, full of shame and anger, staring down at my hands folded on the desk. As if my gaze were a testimony of respect, I withheld it from him. Finally the priest broke the silence. "You must find out what is true about God for yourselves. Arrive at a faith that is deeper than your learning, a faith that rises up from your own depths." He said that we needed to let go of what everyone told us and come up with our own faith, a faith of commitment, a faith based on relationship and experience, a faith that was alive and rooted in our ultimate concerns.

It took a while to understand what he was talking about, but eventually the distinction between faith and religion surfaced. Religion was something that I had inherited, that I was born into and taught. It came to me from the outside. Faith was something that I was being challenged to create from the inside out, something profoundly personal that would stand up to any test because it evolved from my own compassion and commitments.

The lane that ended for me that day was the lane of dependence—dependence on the church, on external authority, on others' concepts and opinions about what is true. The biblical paradox that claims you must lose your life in order to find it started to make sense. I had to give up the known—my programming—which was handed down to me and accepted without challenge, for the unknown, which is the continually unfolding mystery and expression of who I am and what I believe.

Religion is up to others. Faith is up to us. If there were no religions in the world, it wouldn't keep any of us from having an intimate, vital relationship with the Divine, for that relationship is something we create personally, every day. It doesn't take religion to make a person of faith. It takes awareness, compassionate practice, mindful behavior.

Lanes are coming to an end for all of us all the time. Just when we think we're sailing smoothly down the path of life, along comes an upset—we lose a job, a loved one dies, our marriage dissolves, we find out that we have cancer or that our child is on drugs. When the structures around us collapse, our first response is often shock, as the walls of our well-constructed lives come tumbling down. But shock is often the first step in the creation of something new and more beautiful than the old. Shock may be what the caterpillar feels when its safe cocoon breaks open to reveal a remarkable transformation into butterfly nature. Shock may be what the acorn experiences when its shell bursts apart to let loose the unfolding oak within.

Imaginative changes are brought about by shock, experiences that unsettle our whole notion of reality and require that we reconstruct our universe in some new way. In *Moments of Being*, Virginia Woolf writes,

> I suppose that the shock-receiving capacity is what makes me a writer. I feel that I have had a blow; but it is not, as I thought as a child, simply a blow from an enemy hidden behind the cotton wool of daily life; it is or will become a revelation of some order; it is a token of some real thing behind appearances; and I make it real by putting it into words. It is only by putting it into

words that I make it whole; this wholeness means that it has lost its power to hurt me; it gives me, perhaps because by doing so I take away the pain, a great delight to put the severed pieces together. Perhaps this is the strongest pleasure known to me.

When the lane we're on comes to an end, it's time to give up an illusion for the truth that lies beneath it. And this is not a matter of effort. As Deepak Chopra says, "Effort is the problem, not the solution." The only thing we need to do is let go. Our self-understanding is about to undergo a revolution, and we need to stop clinging to the past and let the revolution happen. Instead of asking, "Why is this happening to me?" ask, "Why is this happening *for* me?"

Your own cocoon is splitting open so that your wings can emerge. Just breathe deeply, stay calm, and know that you are evolving every day, just like the rest of the natural world of which you are a part. This is a growth spurt, a step forward.

Every breakthrough is preceded by a breakdown. Every dawn starts at midnight.

Some real thing is behind these appearances: awareness of that reality we are seeking on the spiritual path. We are in search of the Real, and the suffering we experience is tied to our illusions. The only means of transformation in our lives is awareness—awareness of who we are and what is real.

When I was a novice in that theology class, I had no idea who I was or what was real. I knew only what I had been taught, and I could barely stand to question the concepts that supported my life. Mentoring from that priest taught me how to create my own faith, to *put the severed pieces together* and come up with something real and powerful enough—not to die for but to live for.

The hard thing about inherited beliefs is that we think we should defend them. It doesn't occur to us that, as we evolve, our thoughts evolve; as we mature, our spirituality matures. We develop our own worldview. We see how others have shaped our thinking and begin to drop what no longer rings true. We ask ourselves, would I think this way if I was born in China, in Africa? Then we begin to develop, from the inside out, a faith of our own making, based on what it is we believe is true and right and worthy of our commitment.

The Buddha, on his deathbed, said, "Do not accept what you hear by report; do not accept tradition; do not accept a statement because it is found in our books, nor because it is in accord with your belief, nor because it is the saying of your teacher. Be lamps unto yourselves." To be lamps unto ourselves we must claim who we are and create our own creeds from our own depths. No guru, no priest, no mystic can give us truth. They can give us formulas, offer concepts, interpret sacred writings, but these are not truth. They are the menu, not the meal. They are the map, not the journey.

True sages admit that we cannot say anything about the awakened state but can speak only of the sleeping state. St. Thomas Aquinas said about God that "we cannot say what

He is"; we can say only "what He is not." The highest form of knowledge is to know that one does not know, like the Zen master who was asked by a student what happens when you die.

He answered, "I don't know."

"But aren't you a Zen master?" asked the student.

"Yes, but not a dead one."

It is only our *experience* that is real. No one can say what is true for anyone else, for our truth rises up from who we are and what we experience. The Indian poet Kabir writes, "If you have not experienced it, it isn't true." Spirituality is a matter of who we are, of becoming what we are. The spiritual path, then, is a journey into ourselves, into our own divine nature, our own knowing. In the words of Marcel Proust, "We do not receive wisdom, we must discover it for ourselves, after a journey through the wilderness, which no one else can make for us, which no one can spare us, for our wisdom is the point of view from which we come at last to view the world."

So when a lane you are on comes to an end, and you feel the world caving in because what you thought was true no longer appears to be, go into yourself and remember who you are. Remember that you are not your thoughts, not what anyone ever said you were, not what you have tried to construct from your concepts of right and wrong.

You are Infinite Mind. When you look up and see only clouds, remember that above the clouds is infinite sky and that this, too, is you. The shocks you experience are openings into your infinite nature. We get brief glimpses of this so that we do not forget; we get moments of enlightenment so that we know to hang on to the wheel and keep moving forward. There is nothing ahead but the Light.

Yield

The word *yield* has a variety of meanings. On the road, it means to surrender, to give way. In nature, it means to engender, to bear fruit. On the spiritual path, one leads to the other. Once we give up our notion of how life "should be," we free ourselves to experience the abundance of the lives we *do* have.

What keeps many of us from experiencing joy is the illusion that the circumstances of our lives are not right. *If only this thing changed, I could have the life I want, write the book I want to write, have the kind of marriage I desire.* We think if only something changed on the outside, our lives would improve. But that's like being sick and asking the doctor to prescribe something for your neighbor.

Nobody but us is responsible for our happiness. It is our natural state. If we are not happy, it's not because somebody has taken something away from us. It is because we have added something to reality—some illusion, some desire, some attachment to "how it should be." And this is what we have to surrender, this notion that someone else is to blame for what our lives look like.

I know a recovering alcoholic who wakes up every morning, gets on her knees, and waves a white handkerchief in the air. She is surrendering to the reality of who she is, acknowledging what is true for her, and summoning help for her journey. This is what's up for her in this lifetime. She is not going to turn into a nonalcoholic. She's not blaming anyone for who she is. She's not wishing for something that is not, but embracing what *is* in her life, and she's a successful, creative, joyful person because of it.

As true as it is that we create our lives, that our thoughts, words and feelings actually generate the reality we find ourselves in, it is also true that we are in a never-ending dance with its unpredictable particularities—dipping, swaying, bumping, and grinding to the beat of it. Fiction writers and playwrights often talk about the characters they have created taking on lives of their own. While the writers think they know where the characters are headed, the characters themselves often go off in their own independent direction, and the writers' role is to surrender and give way. The creator begins the work and sets the stage, then a door opens in the imagination and surprising things come to life. This is the creative process, not unlike our own lives.

In our lives, we are the playwrights who set the stage. We choose certain careers, relationships, and lifestyles as the backdrop for our creation, and that is the set until we choose something else. What happens on that stage, though, is not always up to us, since it is peopled with individuals who have lives and imaginations of their own. What *is* up to us is how we respond to the action and interact with the other characters and our own inner thoughts. This is the dance we're in, and we get to choose whether we lead or follow.

When we think of yielding or surrendering, it feels more like following than leading, but, in a way, the reverse is true. Whenever we come up against a challenging person or situation, we're often inclined to judge or blame. This happens constantly, on the highway, in the workplace, in the grocery store, in our living rooms and bedrooms. If we feel edgy, we look for someone to blame. *It can't be me that's wrong; it must be them. I would be fine if they would just do this or that. I feel terrible because this situation is all wrong.*

If we follow our instincts, then, we walk right into the illusion that someone or something else is responsible for our feelings. If we surrender that illusion and take control of our thoughts, we take the lead in the dance. Instead of following our feelings, we learn to direct them.

The next time you find yourself disgruntled, check inside to see if there's a voice saying, "It should be *this* way, not that way." If that's the case, give it up. It *is* the way it *is*. Our happiness comes from contact with reality. The more we learn to accept it and flow with it, the happier we become. Trying to change reality, trying to control the behaviors of other people—this is what causes unhappiness. We can create our circumstances, in most cases, and we can control our thoughts and behavior in the context of those circumstances, but as far the great River of Reality we're swimming in, the only choice we have is to swim upstream or down.

The other day I tripped over a book on the floor of a library. It was an old book, called *Children of the Gods*, written by a retired editor whose life was changed by an experience in the Mayan ruins. He had gone to work on an archeological dig and had a preternatural vision telling him that the earth was created in an experiment in altered consciousness by children of higher beings, who then forgot their original awareness.

The book is a record of his experiences, including the voices of several "rememberers" who were trying to retrieve and piece together the truths they once knew. The first rememberer says:

> The truth you seek is hidden by your wish to find it. You are chained to every pain and sorrow by your desire that it shouldn't be happening the way it is. *It is the wanting something else that nearly kills you.* Seek what is at hand. When you give up all your hopes you also give up all your fears. Save yourself, heal yourself, rest yourself in the unexpected. (emphasis mine)

Resting ourselves in the unexpected is not something we're naturally inclined to do. It takes practice, vigilance, awareness of the power of our inner voices to sabotage our calm. Being on the spiritual path means listening intently to these voices, knowing when they're serving us and when they're not, discerning when to yield and when not to.

A friend of mine was planning to build a stone wall in front of her townhouse in Virginia. She drove a Jeep and on Thursday filled the whole back end of it with rocks in preparation for her weekend project. Thursday night, as she drove into the parking lot at 11 p.m., she had a horrifying recollection. She was supposed to pick up three people at the airport on Friday morning. What was she going to do with all the rocks?

She had a moment of choice here, to surrender and make peace with reality or to resist and struggle. She was agitated at first, but finally gave in, opened the tailgate, and in the quiet darkness, unloaded each rock and began to build her stone wall by feel. As she held each rock in her arms, carrying it to its proper place, she felt a kind of calm come over her. "It was just me, the rocks, and the moonlight," she said. "It took three hours to get it done, but once I let go of my anger, the whole process was beautiful."

When she went out the next morning and saw in the light of day what she had built, she was astonished. "It was perfect. A stone mason couldn't have done a better job. I was so proud and amazed—it was almost effortless once I gave up the struggle."

Yielding, while it is not usually our first instinct, is often the best. It is a gracious movement, so much lovelier and softer than steely resistance. It is an act of awareness, a creative gesture that bears fruit, deflects anger, awakens the tenderness within and without. So when you come to that sign in the road, don't try to race ahead, cutting someone off—take your time, remember that woman kneeling with the handkerchief, that stone fence being built in the night: remember the calm, the joy, the grace of surrendering.

Chapter Four

Curves Ahead

Being on a spiritual path pretty much guarantees one thing: the road you are on will never be straight. In that journey from God to GOD, from transcendent faraway God to the immanent Divinity within, one thing remains constant: what's ahead is nothing but Mystery tugging at your ankles, asking over and over, have you *really* let go? We say "Yes!" and the next minute find ourselves saying something that was programmed into us forty years ago.

I was carpooling in an RV with two women from San Diego, heading for Santa Fe, New Mexico, where I was scheduled to lead a weekend workshop. Halfway there, my artist friend Jane announces she's an atheist.

"Jane," I say, "You're going to a workshop called *Divining the Body*. You're going to be the only atheist in the room."

"That's okay. I usually am."

"What do you do when everybody talks about God like they do?"

"Oh, I'm used to it now. You can forget about it. It won't matter."

But I could not forget about it. I drove hundreds of miles pondering how I could make this feel as good for Jane at it was going to feel for everyone else. I didn't want her to feel excluded. I did not want to use language that was foreign to her. My job as a facilitator was to create a sense of oneness, and I had my work cut out for me; that I could see.

We stopped at the Albuquerque airport to pick up three women from Missouri, who started talking about God the moment they arrived. God did this. God did that. Every time I heard the word, my ears burned. I wondered how it felt to have everyone talking as if they had just received a text message from God himself when you had no belief whatsoever in an external Almighty Heavenly Father.

"It was raining, but God got us a great taxi driver who got us there on time."

"I was married to an alcoholic, but God set it up that way so that I'd learn patience."

"God helped me find the right man on eHarmony. . . . God gave me a child with disabilities. . . . God gave me cancer because . . ."

Every time I heard the word *God*, I wanted to say, "Who exactly are you talking about and how does this work?"

We pulled into the parking lot and had two hours before our first gathering. I still had no idea how to handle things, but a thought occurred to me as I entered our meeting room. We sat in a circle and I said to the group, "There's only one rule for the entire weekend. You can share anything you want, but you can't use the word *God*."

"Why not?"

"Because we're trying an experiment—we're trying to take things to a deeper level here, broaden our ways of understanding and expressing our relationship with the Source. If we have to come up with new ways to describe what we're talking about, we'll get clearer about what it really is . . . because we won't be able to fall back on a conceptual word that may not work for everyone in our presence. It's a global world now and we have to practice relating to people who don't necessarily share the same notion of God."

They agreed and we kept the rule all weekend, with just a few little slips. By Sunday lunchtime, an incredible energy surged through our group. Women were grounded in their speaking, and their words radiated self-authority. They claimed their wisdom, shared their journeys, and took full responsibility for the lives they had created. Though it didn't come naturally in the early stages, by the end of the weekend they were pros in communicating their essence. No one had to point to the heavens, abdicate their power, give credit to some God in the sky. Instead, they praised themselves, acknowledged their courage, and claimed the very gifts that the disciples of Jesus failed to claim—their ability to do whatever he had done. The spirituality of each of us was deeply affected that weekend, and it wouldn't have happened if I hadn't experienced that curve in the road, having an atheist in our midst.

Since then, I have tried to discourage people from using the word *God* in my workshops. I try to keep my own language nontheistic and inclusive. In fact, in my morning meditation, I often practice being post-theist, imagining the world without a Supreme Creator. When I started this, I asked myself if I could feel awe if there were no divine Being. I thought of the cosmos without a Creator, this planet spinning on its axis at 1070 miles per hour, orbiting the sun at 67,000 miles per hour. I thought of our solar system tucked away in an arm of the Milky Way, rotating around the galaxy's center at 490,000 miles per hour. "If there's not a God, can I be in awe?" I asked myself. The answer was this:

If there is a God, I am in awe.

If there is *not* a God, I am in greater awe.

The great mystical paleontologist Teilhard de Chardin writes of a similar feeling in his book *Phenomenon of Man*: "If, as the result of some interior revolution, I were to lose in succession my faith in Christ, my faith in a personal God, and my faith in spirit, I feel that I should continue to believe invincibly in the world. The world (its value, its infallibility and its goodness) . . . when all is said and done, is the first, the last, the only thing in which I believe. It is by this faith that I live. And it is to this faith, I feel, that at the moment of death, rising above all doubts, I shall sur-render myself."

To believe invincibly in this world—to help sustain it, to suffer with it, to know our oneness with it—these are all signs of a spiritual evolutionary. As the poet Susan Griffin so beautifully puts it:

> We know ourselves to be made from this earth.
>
> We know this earth is made from our bodies.
>
> For we see ourselves.
>
> And we are nature.
>
> We are nature seeing nature.
>
> We are nature with a concept of nature.
>
> Nature weeping.
>
> Nature speaking of nature to nature.

Ours is not the world of Moses, of Abraham, or even of Jesus. The Babylonians thought they could build a tower to heaven. In medieval times, people thought it would take eight thousand years at forty miles a day by mule to reach the sphere of the stars. In the seventeenth century, Bishop James Ussher calculated time according to Genesis and concluded that the creation of heaven and earth occurred on October 23, 4004 BCE. But wait! Curves Ahead. New facts and findings are changing our minds at lightning speed.

We now know that humans were making art in caves in 290,000 BCE, thousands of years before the concept of God was introduced. Bonobos and humans share 98.7 percent of the same genetic blueprint. Research from HeartMath Institute shows that one person's heart signal can affect another's brainwaves. Monkeys have been trained to control computers with their thoughts. And our planet is moving toward the constellation Leo at the dizzying speed of 242 miles per second.

The old cosmology no longer works. Nor does any mythology based on facts that have long been disproved. So long Garden of Eden. So long Adam and Eve. So long original sin and the need for redemption. You are perfect as you are. You are capable of miracles. You are one with all creation. Follow *these* curves for a while and see where they take you.

CHAPTER FIVE

Divided Highway

We have all been socially conditioned to think dualistically. In fact, we have a major highway running right through the center of our brains, separating the more linear, rational left side from the more imaginative and creative right side. One is not better than the other, any more than left-handed is better than right-handed, black is better than white, Democrat is better than Republican. Recognizing how deeply we are programmed to compare and contrast, to divide and conquer, is an important step on the spiritual path.

I was raised Catholic. Part of our religious training led us to think that only Catholics could get into heaven. Millions of people actually thought this at one time, and this belief led to behavior that could not be classified as either loving or compassionate. My father was not Catholic and it broke my heart to think of him being stuck in purgatory forever.

As a family, we often traveled on the weekends to see my grandparents, who lived sixty miles away. Being in northern New York, in the winter months we often met with blinding blizzards and would have to stop driving when we were only halfway there. Occasionally on a Saturday night, we would be forced off the road because of the snow and would end up at my father's relatives' house. They were not Catholic, and in my badly programmed brain, I thought it was a terrible sin even to walk into their Congregational Church.

When I was twelve years old, I got into a fistfight with a neighbor boy who said that Jesus wasn't born on December 25. For some reason, it seemed worthy of violence to defend that particular date. Most of us can reflect back on teachings we inherited and see the errancy right away. Becoming spiritually mature is a matter of identifying our inherited beliefs and letting go of the ones that no longer serve us. In his preface to *Leaves of Grass*, Walt Whitman writes, "Re-examine all you have been told in school or church or in any book, and dismiss whatever insults your own soul."

Any belief that does not lead to kindness to every person and creature and blade of grass is worthy of being dismissed. Any belief that separates one from another, calling one right and the other wrong, is suspect and deserves to be examined. In 1982, I was planning for a peace pilgrimage around the world. I put a notice in the *Sojourners* magazine bulletin board that I was looking for peace-loving people to stay with in different countries. A few weeks later, I received an envelope from Germany with fourteen pages of legal-size paper containing the names, addresses, and short biographies of like-minded people from a dozen different countries. It was from a man named Amos, who had spent several years in Israel trying to atone for the sins of his father, who had been an SS soldier. He had become a peace activist who worked with both Israelis and Palestinians, and he sent me the names of several families I could stay with.

One night I was in the house of a young Palestinian man named Hossein. It was my last night there, and the whole family had gathered to say farewell. When his father asked where I was going next, I said, "to the house of David and Shoshana." He threw his arms up in the air and yelled, "How can you do this to our family, betray us like this?" The mere fact that I was going to be with an Israeli family felt like a betrayal to him.

This is not original thinking. It is unexamined thinking, socially programmed thinking that leads to the continuation of violence and hatred. All around us are signs of divided highways. The Right has its news station and tells a story one way. The Left has its news station and tells the story another way. We are swimming in a sea of divisiveness, and our first job is to be aware of that. To notice how it plays out every day and to counter it in any way we can. Deepak Chopra has said that our problems lie in the field of diversity, while our solutions lie in the field of unity. The Gnostic Gospel of Thomas quotes Jesus as saying, "When you make the two into one, and when you make the inner as the outer, and the upper as the lower, and when you make male and female into a single one, so that the male shall not be male, and the female shall not be female . . . then you will enter the kingdom."

A Hassidic saying goes as follows: "When the ax comes into the forest, the trees—upon seeing its wooden handle— say, 'Look, one of us.'" It is this kind of deeper noticing that surfaces when one is on the spiritual path. We do not weep and wail. We do not lose our bearings or abandon hope.

We simply notice that we are awash in dualism and strive to *re*-pair the opposites every chance we get.

Retreat director Anthony de Mello often said that it takes the same training to make a terrorist as it does to make a Francis of Assisi. He was speaking of how children are programmed to think. I remember being on my knees when I was twelve years old, praying that God would give me a chance to be martyred for him. I sincerely wanted to die for my faith.

Many of us survived and outgrew the brainwashing we received as children. We have grown ourselves up spiritually and emotionally, trusting our intuition and our body's wisdom to be our moral compass. We no longer believe something just because somebody else claims it is true. We believe what we believe because of our lived experience, out of our *own* authority. We are the authors of our own spirituality, living up to the words of the Buddha, who said, "Do not believe in anything simply because you have heard it. Do not believe in anything simply because it is spoken and rumored by many. Do not believe in anything simply because it is found written in your religious books. Do not believe in anything merely on the authority of your teachers and elders. Do not believe in traditions because they have been handed down for many generations. But after observation and analysis, when you find that anything agrees with reason and is conducive to the good and benefit of one and all, then accept it and live up to it."

Even the Dalai Lama admits that his religion is human kindness. That makes it easy. Nothing to memorize. Nothing to argue over. Nothing to die for. Just one simple practice: to see that you live in a world that tries to keep us divided and to do everything in your power to reconnect what you see torn asunder.

End Divided Highway

A while ago, I was asked to give a short talk at the opening reception at a hospital where four doctors were exhibiting their photographs. The woman who invited me to speak did so because I have a book entitled *God Is at Eye Level: Photography as a Healing Art,* and she thought it was a good connection. A few days before the opening she called to say, "A couple of the doctors are upset because they don't want anyone bringing religion into the picture. They say their photography has nothing to do with healing. So be careful what you say."

I arrived at the reception early enough to view all the photographs and was moved by each body of work. One was a series of black-and-white images from the same Himalayan mountain range in which I had trekked a decade earlier. One group was color landscapes from my favorite place in this country, Canyon de Chelley on the Navajo reservation in Arizona. One was an array of close-ups of flowers, and another was a series of vibrant murals and portraits from a Hispanic barrio in south San Diego. Every photograph in the exhibition spoke to my heart, aroused my emotions, and awakened my joy.

When I started to talk, I looked out at the doctors, their arms crossed, their faces stern and inanimate. I was mindful of speaking only about my own process of photographing, not wanting to make any of them uncomfortable. I spoke about photography as my way of grounding myself in the present, about how it's the most healing thing I do because it roots me in the now, and, when I'm there, I feel a oneness with life. I'm untouched and unfettered by anything past or future—no regrets, no fears, no anxieties—just a kinship with what's at hand. I spoke of my belief that the Divine dwells in the present moment, and, when I'm there, I feel safe and secure.

I shared my reactions to each of the doctor's photographs, commenting on how they awakened my senses, conjured up memories, ignited my imagination and joy. Their images made me feel connected to my world, in awe of its mystery, in love with its flowering. And this, to me, was a holy thing because it made me feel *whole*. And when we *feel* whole, we speak with our whole heart, and what emanates from our being then is a love and authenticity that breaks through every obstacle on its way to the heart of another. Or as Coleman Barks so poetically puts it, "All the particles of the world are in love and looking for lovers. Pieces of straw tremble in the presence of amber."

As I spoke, I watched the doctors move forward in their seats. I saw their faces soften, their eyes widen. They never knew the power of their work, the healing potential of their images. They never knew that something they created had the power to bring another into wholeness, but when I spoke of it, when they could see that my energy had been affected by their work, something shifted in their thinking. After the talk, one doctor came up to me, took me aside, and said, "I could never talk about spirituality in my practice before, but your talk opened something up for me. I saw you come alive when you spoke about the spiritual, about how our photographs actually moved you. It was like a light going off. Your honesty was so compelling and it made me wonder, 'Why do I need to keep that part of me locked up?' I don't think I do anymore."

In turn, the other doctors approached me, one at a time, and said very similar things. They were afraid to talk of the sacred, afraid to use the G-word, afraid that they might be misunderstood, so they kept silent in the matter. For all those years they had followed the rules without questioning, but that evening opened a chink in the wall and another possibility came into being.

Being committed to your spiritual path causes a shift in consciousness that results in a new way of being and acting in the world. It leads to *embodied* insight. It does not happen because we will it or work for it. It comes gratuitously when we clear the passageways between our minds and our hearts, when we trust and act upon our bodies' messages, and when we master the art of transcending duality, which means simply that instead of resisting what appears to be "other" we embrace it, bring it into ourselves, and see what transpires when the poles unite. Jungian psychologist and scholar Marie-Louise von Franz writes: "If we can stay with the tension of opposites long enough—sustain it, be true to it—we can sometimes become vessels within which the divine opposites come together and give birth to a new reality."

All our lives we have been trained to look for differences, to rebel against ideas that are the opposite of our own, to seek out people who are like ourselves. Who is "the enemy" but someone whose ideas are contrary to ours? This is ordinary thinking, and it has gotten us just where we are today. Re-examining our thoughts is the only thing that will transport us beyond our current state, and that calls for discipline and practice. Original thinking is a process that seeks out the opposite in order to incorporate it, to understand it, to embody it, knowing that a fusion of the two is what creates the new.

The poet Baudelaire said that "true genius is the ability to hold two contradictory thoughts simultaneously without losing your mind." This is step one in the process of transcending duality. You won't lose your mind, but you do have to *use* your mind. Just as we have to exercise and retrain our muscles after periods of nonuse, so do we need to exercise and retrain our minds when they have atrophied into a state of habitual duality. When new learning occurs, it literally changes the architecture of the human brain; hence, the catchphrase "neurons that fire together, wire together" is well-established in developmental neuroscience. What we're doing when we unite opposites is literally rewiring our brains. We are creating new neural networks, new pathways in the brain that will reroute us from knee-jerk reactions to heart-based responses.

Ideas that are born from the union of thought and feeling, that originate out of a desire for synthesis and a diligence to rise above duality contain within themselves the DNA of transcendence. Carl Jung called emotion the chief source of consciousness. "There is no change from darkness to light or from inertia to movement without emotion," he writes. The practice of uniting opposites involves opening the heart as much as the mind. It means feeling our way forward even as we're thinking our way forward, for it is our feelings that rise up like red lights, alerting us to the crossroads of old habits and new choices.

There is a momentary discomfort as we try to find the rightness in another's thinking or perceive the "enemy" as our self. It goes against everything we've ever learned, and it involves the same kind of emotional withdrawal symptoms that come with every attempt to give up an addiction. We are addicted to dualism because every institution of our lives has promoted this kind of thinking, but none of us can call ourselves free until we have rid ourselves of this dangerous habit. The ability to hold two contradictory thoughts simultaneously is not just a matter of true genius; it is a matter of true freedom. If we cannot hear an opposing idea without a negative emotional reaction, we are not free. We are bound to an ideology that we have most likely inherited and never thoroughly examined.

Just as a battery is charged by the union of positive and negative forces, just as a child is conceived by the union of a male sperm and female ovum, just as a thought issues forth from the union of right and left brain, so does our authentic spirituality emerge from the practice of joining "us" and "them" into a "we." Our imaginations are the most potent engines of change in the universe, and when we change our thought patterns and become conscious of our speaking, we will make a quantum leap forward on our spiritual path.

Being in touch with our emotions is an essential part of this practice. They are our guide, our body's means of *instant messaging* to the brain. *Yes, this decision is wise. No, that choice is unwise.* Our bodies are hardwired for survival of the species, and if we listen deeply to them, if we are wise enough to trust the feelings they emanate on our behalf, then we will find the clarity necessary to make inspired choices that are as good for the whole as they are for the one. And because the work of transforming our own thought processes is so evolutionary an act, it requires the total engagement of body, mind, and spirit. This is not business as usual. This is reorienting to a new star.

Parts of us will balk at the letting go of the old, but it is the only way forward. And when we feel our emotions ruffling at this new attempt toward unity, we should rejoice, for it is a sign that we are fully alive and engaged in the great work of transformation—personal at first, but ultimately global.

Transformation is like the opening of a prison door, allowing us to see what we could not see before because we were locked into certain beliefs and habits. Millions of women experienced this during the days of consciousness raising, when they suddenly realized that the personal is political; that who they were and how they felt about themselves was shaped by cultural, political, and religious institutions that benefited from keeping women in certain roles. It wasn't until women started meeting in small groups and sharing their stories that they discovered that the problem was more external than internal and as systemic as it was local. "The enemy has outposts in our heads," was an oft-repeated phrase.

Women's very thought processes had been infected, and the remedy was twofold. First came the telling of the stories, the careful listening, the making of incremental shifts from self-censorship to self-expression and to self-awareness and self-determination. Next came the action, the mobilization, the campaigns to equalize power and bring some yin to the yang of the corporate and cultural table.

This action, of course, met with resistance, and the media made a mockery of these women, whose resolve to create a better world for everyone was belittled and undermined by such phrases as "bra burners" and "angry feminists." Forty years later, many women hesitate to call themselves "feminists," because that very term is a label that pushes buttons and puts up walls, but it cannot be denied that what came to life out of those living-room gatherings—out of all the stories and sobs and anger and disenchantment—was a full-blown social movement that led to an overhaul of American consciousness.

And it is this kind of transformation, this kind of social evolution, that we are in the midst of now, though it is more oblique, more implicit and unquantified, because it is happening in the inner milieu of ideas, values, perceptions, emotions. As a culture, we have not developed many tools for measuring the inner realms, though it is there that every movement for change is conceived and gestates until it is delivered into the world as an embodied idea, an independent force with its own shape and substance.

In the late 1990s, a number of various social organizations came together in protest against global trade agreements that they feared would exploit the poor and harm the earth. What drove them together was a shared value, a commitment to keep the body politic and our home planet from harm. They were not against profit, not against progress or the international exchange of technology and talent. They were taking a stand against thoughtlessness, against greed, against the implementation of regulations that might pave the way for corporate abuse or irresponsibility.

To cite an example from nature, their actions were akin to the oyster's, when a foreign substance, such as a grain of sand, enters its body. To protect its soft inner body against intrusion, the oyster takes defensive action, and its cells secrete a smooth and hard substance, called nacre, around the irritant. This nacre is composed of microscopic crystals, and because each crystal is aligned perfectly with every other one, the light passing along the axis of one is reflected and refracted by the others to produce a rainbow of light and color. For years, the oyster continues to secrete this crystalline substance around the irritant, until the irritant is totally encased and ultimately transformed into a lustrous gem called a pearl.

The protesters were like the nacre, bringing their consciousness to bear on deliberations that could affect the lives of billions of people. As they circled the building where the trade agreements were being discussed, they were encasing the irritant, which was, to them, an imbalance of representation and a governing body with no checks or balances. What they were calling for was inclusion in the conversation, the ability to add "people" and "the planet" to an agenda they feared was solely about "profit."

If we carry the analogy further, imagining these protesters as those microscopic crystals, aligning perfectly, passing their light along from one to another, reflecting and refracting ideas in such a way that they become a rainbow of luminous thought, then we can envision the possibility of this light force transforming what was once an "irritant" into a "pearl of great price." It is this kind of imagining that surfaces in the act of nondualistic thinking. There is no longer the old "we're right, they're wrong" conclusion, but a stretching into wholeness that surpasses duality. Unitive thinking employs the opposites; it starts with duality but doesn't stop until it has brought the two forces together, culminating in a creative combustion that dissolves dissonance and creates a higher order.

Transformation ushers forth from the reconciliation of opposites. What caused the shift in thinking for the doctor photographers? When they came into the room, they were stone-faced and resolute, resistant to the notion that their work had anything to do with healing or spirituality. When

I talked about the impact of their work on me, I said how healing it was *because* it moved me spiritually and emotionally. And because I talked about my feelings, they trusted and believed me—their work *was* healing and it *did* have a spiritual quality. The unfolding of this awareness was what caused their bodies to relax, their faces to loosen up. What they thought was not true, was. While they did not intend for their images to be healing or to have spiritual value, they were and they did. This collision of their own expectations with my response to their work sparked a transformation not just in their minds but in their bodies and actions; each of them mentioned it and thanked me for it.

Ending our divided highways is a lifelong pursuit. It means taking a stand. It means being clear about your commitments and acting on them day after day. It is noble, necessary work, and it is being done round the clock, around the globe by all your fellow citizens who are on the spiritual path.

Falling Rocks Ahead

The danger of creating and staying true to your own spiritual path is that you may be accused of wrongdoing by others who are following traditional and unexamined routes. As you are attempting to think anew and remain true to your inner wisdom, some may challenge you with biblical passages or dogmatic beliefs. Your job here is to have a response that is both honest and loving. You could say something like,

"I'm with the Dalai Lama. My new religion is human kind-ness." Or perhaps you could try, "I'm simplifying my religion. I'm just sticking with the Golden Rule."

The important thing is not to defend your action as if your way is right and their way is wrong. It's nobody's busi-ness but yours what your spiritual path looks like or where it takes you. That said, it is often helpful to others when you openly share where your journey is taking you. So many mil-lions of us are evolving ourselves, moving forward step by step, and it is helpful to be in communion with others who are blazing their own trails.

A few years ago, I received an e-mail from Episcopal Bish-op John Shelby Spong. I have read all his books and cherish the contributions he has made to my own spiritual growth. In his e-mail manifesto, he wrote:

I have made a decision. I will no longer debate the issue of homosexuality in the church with anyone. I will no longer engage the biblical ignorance that emanates from so many right-wing Christians about how the Bible condemns homosexuality, as if that point of view still has any credibility. I will no longer discuss [this subject] with them or listen to them tell me how homosexuality is 'an abomination to God,' about how homosexuality is a 'chosen lifestyle,' or about how through prayer and 'spiritual counseling' homosexual persons can be 'cured.' Those arguments are no longer worthy of my time or energy. I will no longer dignify by listening to the thoughts of those who advocate 'reparative therapy,' as if homosexual persons are somehow broken and need to be repaired. I will no longer talk to those who believe that the unity of the church can or should be achieved by rejecting the presence of, or at least at the expense of, gay and lesbian people.

It went on for seventeen hundred words and ended with "This is my manifesto and my creed. I proclaim it today.

I invite others to join me in this public declaration." Who knows what kind of risk this was for him, or what amount of bravery it took, or what the pushback was from the official church. We can never know that, but what we can know is how much his words matter—how reconciling they are, how healing and evolutionary. There's something about another's courage that is contagious. After I read Spong's proclamation, I got an e-mail from a friend in Ohio who announced to her mailing list the following: "I'm done being Christian. I can't buy into the message anymore. Every religion is the true religion to the one who believes in it."

My good friend, a nun for forty-seven years, said to me about attending Mass, "I can't go to those deadening rituals anymore. They have no life. They don't feed my soul." One in ten Americans is an ex-Catholic; if they were counted as their own religious group, ex-Catholics would be the third-largest denomination in the United States after Catholics and Baptists, according to the *National Catholic Reporter*. I researched the reasons so many Catholics were leaving the church. CNN's Belief Blog reports that, in a study done by two university professors, when three hundred non-churchgoing Catholics in Trenton, New Jersey, were asked why they left the church, these were their top seven reasons: the sex-abuse crisis, the anti-gay stance, dissatisfaction with priest, uninspiring homilies, the official church's conservative nature, the church's position on divorced and remarried Catholics, the low status of women (http://religion.blogs.cnn.com/2012/03/30/7-reasons-catholics-leave-church-in-trenton-1-is-sex-abuse-crisis/).

Pierre Berton, in his book *The Comfortable Pew*, a look at the Anglican Church in 1960s Canada (cited at http://inaspaciousplace.wordpress.com/2012/07/05/the-comfortable-pew-a-few-problems/), reported that people were leaving because the liturgies failed to have any relevance or emotional impact:

Many people who no longer attend church, but who continue to call themselves Christian, give as a reason the fact that the service "does nothing for them." The liturgy is "dull and old-fashioned," the phraseology unfamiliar, the words archaic, the sermons cliche-ridden and irrelevant to the times, the organ music "square," the congregation spiritless.

My friend Kathy and her husband, both cradle Catholics, said the other day, "We're trying out the Episcopal Church now. We've looked everywhere in Syracuse for a Catholic Church that's a good fit, but we can't find one."

These sentiments show a degree of spiritual maturity that is refreshing. The people who express them are not just following the flock. They are looking for a community and a church experience that are emotionally satisfying, relevant, and compassionate. And if they don't find this, they will find a way to express their living faith in the real world.

One challenge for the faithful pilgrims who are forging ahead independently, who may have left their churches for the sake of integrity, is the challenge of fulfilling the role of priest and sacrament maker in the everyday world. The thing that transforms our faith into a living, cellular, pulsating experience is the rituals we cocreate—those events that take us out of time, out of our isolation, into the community of souls where we know our oneness, evoke the Creative Source, reconcile our differences, and bestow blessings all around.

We are the sacrament makers of these times, the priests of the imagination who blend music, image, and word into ceremonies that call forth our magnitude and celebrate the mysteries of life and death. Last year I taught a class in evolutionary creativity. I gave everyone in the class an opportunity to have all our attention for fifteen minutes. They could use that time in any way they wanted. Here's one example:

On this night, it is Jalene's turn. Jalene is in her mid-thirties, with long dark hair, a lean, healthy body, and a face as radiant as the sky at dawn. We're sitting in a horseshoe shape—

sixteen of us—and she lays out four flamenco dresses on the floor in the center. Her hair is tied back in a bun, and she wears a red necklace, red earrings, and a brilliant red comb in her hair. There's a flower in her hair, and she is wearing a Spanish flamenco tiered skirt. She hands me two CDs and asks me to play them when I get her cue.

Jalene shares with us the story of the first time she walked through her fear, boarded a plane for Spain, and spent a year there learning flamenco. She speaks for a while of her personal journey; then she begins to tell us about becoming pregnant and the joy it brought to her and her husband. She speaks of the attention they gave to the decision to get pregnant and of the many ways she prepared herself through following months—the yoga, the massages, the foods she ate, and the music she played, always with the hope that the little one would like it. She searched throughout the city for two midwives she trusted, and the day finally came for the child to be born.

Jalene's voice cracks here as she speaks of her son's death at the moment of birth—a tragedy that occurred only three months ago. His name was Elan Vie, from the Hebrew and French for the tree of life, the passion of life. As she stands there before us, she wraps her arms around herself and cries and cries. Tears are flying from her eyes. Those of us in our seats lean forward in rapt and focused compassion, witness to a mystery unfolding before us. Many of us cry right along with her, men and women both wiping tears from our eyes.

When the sorrow abates, she cues me for the music and begins to dance her evolutionary creative art piece. The music is traditional Sevillanas festive music, filled with light and joy. Jalene whirls her way around the group, stopping long enough in front of each of us to make a connection that is deep and dear. After two minutes of flamenco, the lights go down and the music changes to *Grace* by Snatam Kaur.

Jalene spreads her white shawl as an altar cloth on the floor, placing upon it a candle and a copper bowl. She fills the bowl with water from her bottle, bows down, and re-moves her earrings, her necklace, and the red comb from her hair. As she unpins her hair, long dark curls cascade down her back. Jalene bows again before the altar, blesses the water, and pours it over her head. The water splashes down her hair and shoulders, falling like teardrops into her lap and onto her skirt. The moment is sacred. Nobody moves. On her knees still, she bends over in sorrow and begins to sob.

Her sorrow moves around us like a fog rolling in. Each of us feels her grief as we breathe in the air. The strings and piano offer their comfort. The walls and the windows watch in agony. When Jalene's sobs subside, we turn down the lights and sit still in the silence while her pain makes its way through our hearts.

I kneel next to Jalene and ask if she will permit us to keen out our sorrow, a Gaelic tradition of vocal lament in which women at the graveside moan and wail. Jalene nods and we turn the lights completely off. I lie down on the floor, with my head on my arms. Then I begin to wail and cry. Others follow, and people move from their chairs down to the floor. The room is dark. The wailing is deep. The sound of our mourning cannot be described.

When the keening stops of its own accord, I lean over to wrap my arms around Jalene and feel in the dark several hands already there, stroking her back, rubbing her shoulders and water-blessed head. Hardly a body is left in the seats, as we have gravitated toward the center and the source of the pain. Our hands and arms intermingle as one, as we reach out to comfort this childless mother. We are like cells in a body, coming to the aid of a part that is wounded. Moving in the dark, on our bellies and knees, we lean into the hurt one, reaching out in love.

When the sound dies down and the lights come up, the sight of us together is a vision in itself—sprawled out in a circle around the grieving mother, we are petals to the rose of her, channels for her tears. We stand up in silence, hold each other in wonder, and look long and deeply into each other's teary eyes.

While we mourned the loss of a baby that night, we gave birth to something new—birth to an awareness of the power of ritual, and birth to a sacred circle that will never be the same.

Four days later, I attended Sunday services at the Unity Center where we meet for class. When I walked toward the sanctuary, I saw a huddle of people gathered in a circle. It was us! Still in awe, still whirling, still speechless . . . but in love with one another on the heels of that grace.

The following Wednesday, when we met for class, I asked if anyone wanted to share how our experience had affected them during the week. Roy said that he had never seen anyone be so vulnerable in front of others before, and it helped him feel less afraid about sharing his feelings. Allie, Jalene's mother, said that the ritual contained all of the sacraments, from baptism to last rites, including her daughter's ordination as a high priestess, and that it felt like we were all one in the universal womb. Martha had never been in such uncharted territory before, and she felt that the whole ceremony was a communion service. Jennifer said that it felt like Jalene went through the fire and came out a phoenix, and like she was a midwife to each of us doing the same. Katy sensed an expansion of oneness she'd never felt before. David felt as if we had all been bonded in some holy way. Burt felt honored to reach that level of intimacy in a group.

It had been transformative for each of us, as sacred ceremonies are meant to be. And the reason is that every one of us was engaged in the moment, 100 percent present, driven only by an urge to heal and to witness. We were co-celebrants in a sacrament of public grieving. The spontaneity of it was important; the fearlessness was important; the darkness was important; the tenderness and the wailing were important.

This is why there is no official rulebook for the celebration of rituals we are creating these days. We must be present.

We must trust that Spirit will move us in all the appropriate ways. We must be there for and with one another, ready to dissolve boundaries and bestow blessings. The grace is in the movement of Spirit; the creative combustion; the risk of being real, vulnerable, and original. One has to be open. Spirit flies in through open windows.

Chapter Eight

Workers Ahead

Many people think that the spiritual path is an arduous one that requires a lot of effort and hard work. Actually, the opposite is true. A certain discipline is required, but think of that discipline as coming from the word *disciple*. It has to do with love and commitment, not punishment.

My name for the spiritual path is the *Joy Trail*. If I find myself stressed or aggravated, I know I've wandered off the path. Joy is our default mode. Scientists say we're hardwired for bliss. It's just that our software is corrupt and in need of an upgrade. This is a matter of consciousness. We forget that we are already one with whatever we are seeking, that there is no place to get to, that wherever we are, divinity resides. When you are truly on the spiritual path, you come to a complete knowing that all boundaries between you and the Creator are obliterated. You do not have to gain anything to find enlightenment. You have to let go of the idea that you are *not* enlightened. The mystic Meister Eckhart said that God is found in the soul not by adding anything but by a process of subtraction.

What we need to subtract, eliminate, get rid of once and for all are all those notions that the Beloved is somewhere out there, unattainable. What's true is that the force we are seeking, the Creative Source we hunger for, is unavoidable. It is coursing through our veins every minute of the day. It is what is breathing us, what is pumping our hearts. It is *in* us, like the salt in the sea. That power, that force and immensity, is too ineffable, too unbounded to be contained in anything as rigid as a religion. Religions, on a good day, may point to it, but the Light Itself is streaming through seven billion human beings at this very moment. It is the Universe expanding, Creation continuing through our thoughts, our love, the work of our hands. We are the breath, the eyes, the hands of God—and our work today, as human beings, is to know this, to live from this, to fulfill this. And it *is* work, because it involves a commitment to evolving our own consciousness, which requires dedication and discipline. We must mind our thoughts, be cautious with our words, for those are the tools with which we manifest reality.

My best friend in high school became a chief executive for a multinational company in Australia. When I went to visit her she talked about how sad it was that she couldn't be friends with any of her employees. She felt so isolated. I had started a few businesses in the States and said to her that they had been successful *because* I had made friends with every employee. Her response was that in big business you just couldn't do that. "You can't be personal with people you supervise." That, to me, was an example of an illusion, an inherited notion, a handed-down tradition. She honored it like it was a holy corporate commandment, and perhaps it was. But organizations are living things, like evolving organisms. They thrive only when they adapt to their changing environments.

In fact, the latest research on workers and motivation disproves theories we have held true for centuries. Daniel Pink's latest book, *Drive: The Surprising Truth About What Motivates Us*, points out that offering rewards as incentives to workers tends to have a substantially negative effect on intrinsic motivation. Groups that were incentivized by cash rewards took longer to solve creative problems. After analyzing fifty-one studies of corporate pay-for-performance plans, four research economists concluded that higher incentives led to worse performance. "We find that financial incentives . . . can result in a negative impact on overall performance."

Pink also refers to a study done by Harvard Business School professor Teresa Amabile, one of the world's leading researchers of creativity. She and two colleagues recruited twenty-three professional artists who had produced both commissioned and noncommissioned work. The artists were asked to submit ten random commissioned works and ten random noncommissioned works to a panel of accomplished artists and curators who knew nothing about the study. The panel was then asked to rate the pieces on creativity and technical skill. The researchers were quite surprised by the results. It turns out that the panel of experts found the commissioned works to be significantly less creative than the noncommissioned pieces. Said one artist, "Not always, but a lot of the time when you are doing a piece for someone else it becomes more work than joy." People want to create on their own terms, in their own time, for their own reasons, and money will never diminish that desire.

Volunteers around the world have created the most innovative tools for global communication and are working day and night to improve them—not for financial gain, but for the benefit of the human family. *That* is what inspires and motivates them. Think of Linux, Wikipedia, Firefox, and all the open-source software you have benefited from in so many areas—open-source cookbooks, photo sites, medical research, textbooks. Think of Khan Academy and its mission: "A free world-class education for anyone anywhere."

We live in the best of times and the worst of times, and people on the spiritual path are just like everyone else, minus the illusions. Anthony de Mello taught that all our negative emotions are caused by illusions that we allow to obstruct our thinking. If we are sad or angry, it's because there is some underlying illusion preempting our natural state of joy. He says: "When the eye is unobstructed, the result is seeing;

when the ear is unobstructed, the result is hearing; when the palate is unobstructed, the result is tasting. When the mind is unobstructed, the result is wisdom and happiness. Drop your attachments and you will be free. Understand your illusions and they will drop."

It is awareness, not effort, that dissolves the illusions. When we experience an upset, if we look to see what underlying belief or attachment is behind it, we can begin to see what illusions have us in their grip. If I make the mistake of thinking someone else is responsible for my happiness, I'll discover this when I back up and begin to explore my negative feelings about that person's behavior. Why am I upset? Because he didn't do so-and-so. Why should he have done so-and-so? Because it would have made me happy, and he's responsible for my happiness. That is my illusion.

I was in India during the monsoon season, living in a community founded by a man who'd lived many years with Mahatma Gandhi. One morning I woke up to discover that this was the day we were going to begin the construction of a barn. Women, men, and children were forming a line from the creek bed to the site of the building, about a quarter of a mile away. Teenage girls were assembling at the site, where there was a pile of huge rocks. As I took my place in the line, I asked Nayan Bala, the woman next to me, what in the world was going on.

"We're transporting the mortar materials from the creek," she said, as the first tin bowl came my way. "Here, pass this on." The bowl contained a little water, some gravel and small pebbles. I passed it to the woman next to me, and as soon as I turned around, there was another bowl coming at me. I handed that one over and another one came. And another, and another.

It was ninety-eight degrees, and the humidity was hovering at about 95 percent. After passing bowls for an hour, I thought I might like to change places with the girls up at the site. "What are they doing with the big rocks?" I asked. "They carry them on their heads and deliver them to the men once the mortar is in place," said Nayan Bala, passing me another bowl. I decided to stay in line. But the heat was unbearable, and I was getting irritable.

There has to be another way, I thought, as I scanned the horizon looking for some way out of this predicament. I saw several oxen lazing around farther down the creek, a tractor off in the distance, and a flatbed trailer up near the rock pile. "This is ridiculous!" I said to Nayan Bala, whose face was as drenched with sweat as mine. "Why don't we hook up those oxen to some carts and get that tractor hitched to the flatbed. There's no reason why all these people have to be killing themselves passing these little bowls. Let's mechanize this process. *Don't you know that time is money*?"

As much as I'd prided myself on not being an "ugly American," there it was, right out in the open. Even as those last few words tumbled out of my sorry mouth, I knew I had crossed some boundary, creating some new cultural divide with the power of my own words. I wanted to shrink into nonexistence. But Nayan Bala was a mountain of kindness. She put down the bowl that was coming my way, wiped her hands on her sari, and placed them on my shoulders.

"Maybe you haven't been in India long enough to understand something important about us. Every person is in line here because they want to be. In ten years or twenty years, when this barn is built, they will bring their children here, their grandchildren here, and they will tell them the story of how they helped build this barn. They are proud to be doing this, and they will be proud every time they tell the story. Do you think we should deny them this?"

That was the moment for me when I was forced to let go of an existing belief. Time wasn't money for these people— nor for me, actually. That concept was an illusion I had carried with me like an extra bag on my journey. It was an illusion that led to stress and anger. It didn't serve me. It wasn't mine, really. It was an inherited thought, not an original one.

I was simply thinking something I was taught to think. It was the American way, but not the right way—not for this time and place.

Nayan Bala's graciousness allowed me to look at my thoughts and see that they weren't mine at all. But it took an upset like that to set me apart from my own thinking. According to philosopher and integral theorist Ken Wilber, when we are looking at our thoughts we're not using them to look at the world, so there is a moment of freedom there, a moment to be open to a new awareness. Is this thought really mine? Am I the author of it? Has it passed the test of my own experience? The poet Kabir writes, "If you haven't experienced it, it's not true." We can speak powerfully only from our own experience.

Being a spiritually mature person means having to move and think and speak from our own personal knowing. Our power comes from our ability to transform what we have felt into what we know. It's an alchemy of sorts, by which we acquire the skill of transforming the lead of our experience into the gold of our wisdom. Each of us knows what no one else knows because no one else has lived our lives, seen what we have seen, felt what we have felt. The great Persian poet Rumi writes, "The throbbing vein will take you further than any thinking." This is a great clue.

In his book *Conscious Acts of Creation,* physicist William Tiller writes, "As we proceed along the path of inner self-management, structural changes occur within us that allow a significant increase in the level of indwelling spirit and this, in turn, appears as a significant increase in one's level of consciousness." Being on a spiritual path is a process of inner self-management. Once we become adept at managing our thoughts and being aware of every word we speak, we experience an actual increase in our awareness of the Immanent One within us. This is the expansion of our consciousness.

And while it involves commitment and discipline, it is not arduous. It is not a marathon, not an Olympic competition. It is a daily practice. You raise your consciousness day by day. You evolve yourself consciously. You become different—deeper, more joyful, more calm.

Remember this if your practice starts to feel like an effort:

A Zen student goes to the temple to become enlightened.

"I want to join the community and attain enlightenment. How long will it take me?" he asks.

"Ten years," says the Master.

"How about if I work very hard and double my efforts?"

"Twenty years."

Merge

A monk is walking down a mountain path in winter when he falls off the side into a huge snowbank. He tries and tries to get up, but cannot. Later, another monk comes down the trail and sees him. He climbs down into the snowbank and lies next to the monk who has been stranded. At this point the first monk gets up and climbs easily out of the snowbank.

What does this story say to you? Are you confused by its message? Maybe this example will shine some light on it. A number of years ago there was a study at the University of Wisconsin in which subjects were to place a bare foot in a bucket of ice water. The researchers timed how long each subject could keep his or her foot in the bucket. Then they repeated the experiment, but the second time they brought another person into the room as a witness. What the researchers noticed was that when there was a witness present in the room, the person could keep his or her foot in the bucket twice as long.

Having another person present to our pain doubles our capacity to endure it. Once the first monk knew he was not alone, he had the strength to get out of the snowbank. Talking is not needed. Strength is not needed. Wisdom is not needed. It's simply our presence that can help another get through grief or a grueling experience. But what *is* it that makes it so hard for us to *be* there for someone? Why do we feel we need to give advice, or be humorous, or fill up any empty space with meaningless chatter? And what keeps us from being good listeners?

I have a minister friend who spends much of his time engaged with his church families and their problems. He is with them at births and deaths, baptisms and funerals, church suppers and Little League picnics. I do my best to maintain a relationship with him but have noticed over the years that we are sometimes together for two hours and he never inquires into my life. He dominates every conversation with stories about himself and never asks me a question about what's going on in my life.

As a result, I tend to see him less and less, which makes him feel discounted. He said to me last summer, "When you come here, you always rush right off and never have any time for a real visit. When are you going to stop by when you have some time for me?"

I hardly knew what to say, as I didn't want to hurt his feelings by telling him he was a terrible listener. I thought about it for a couple weeks and realized that I owed him my honesty at the very least, so I set up a lunch date to share my feelings with him. I told him how I felt when he talked about himself without ever inquiring about me. I told him that I wanted to have a conscious and mature relationship with him and that meant he had to be a good communication partner. I asked him if he was willing to pay attention when we were together, to help us create a dialogue together, to ask me a question every once in a while. I asked if he would try to discern the balance of male and female voices in the conversation and correct it when it became imbalanced.

While he wasn't jumping for joy, he was grateful to know why I had made myself scarce and what he could do to keep that from happening again. This is the kind of intimacy and authenticity that is required for us to find and keep our partners and companions on the spiritual path. The work we are up to is huge, and unless you are an extraordinary introvert or hermit, you will benefit from others just as the rest of us do.

We are in the process of un-brainwashing ourselves. We are rewiring our neural networks with new thoughts and new behaviors. We are learning how to create our days with intentional thoughts and supportive speaking. We are refusing to accept that life is happening *to* us and we are some victim of circumstance. We are, in large part, creating our own circumstances, all the while knowing we are in a dance with the Invisible Forces that will always be sending learning experiences our way.

Think of it like this: Your soul, before it took on a body, knew it was coming here for a reason. It had a mission. But in the process of being born, in that long journey down the birth canal, it forgot. And there was no one here to remind your soul why it had come. People said it was about money, or buying things, or living in exotic places, or being the right size or age or color. The soul vaguely knew that was not the reason and still longed to recall its mission. The only time it got a faint memory of its mission was when the soul felt deep joy or a tingling of bliss when it was doing a particular thing.

The soul invited big adventures into her life. "Bring me experience," she cried. "Bring me encounters and events from which I can learn. Maybe then I will remember." Experiences and adventures came her way daily—some she called disasters, some she called calamities or catastrophes—but each one was *for* her. They were all her teachers and guides so that she could remember. Every troublesome incident gave her something, added to her insight, bolstered her intuition. Finally one day, when she understood this, she outgrew her suffering and realized *that* was what she had come to do—to help people see that we suffer only until we realize all our experiences are *for* us. They are grist for our creative mills. They are the seeds of our wisdom, the words that become the sentences that become the stories that become the light we are to the darkness around us.

Every person on the spiritual path understands this. They merge with everything and feel at one with all creation. They remove obstacles from every relationship so that the communion and communication are pure and profound. They let go and let go and let go a thousand times, till there is nothing left but the One within and the One in front. They see light everywhere. They rejoice in paradox. They do not defend their ideas or positions but welcome other thoughts to complement their own.

People on the spiritual path are attentive and engaged. They help one another, like the monk in the snowbank. We need one another because our work is countercultural and we always meet with resistance. Our self-authority frightens some people. Others who still belong to traditional religions may feel that we are going down some dangerous road. But that is not true.

What does feel true, to many of us who have left our churches for the sake of integrity, is that we have no home. No spiritual home. No place to go for rituals that sustain us, inspire us, fill us with grace and energy. To some, it feels like we are wandering in the desert. But let us not forget Havelock

Ellis's words, "Paradise always lies on the other side of the wilderness."

This is our time to merge with fellow pilgrims, to cocreate *new* sacraments and ceremonies that evoke the Great Spirit, bring us to our knees in awe and joy, shake us and awaken us with rattles and drums, and give us a chance to give praise and thanks in a common circle. We are the prophets and mystics of these times. The second coming is *us* coming into a higher consciousness, awakening to our own divinity, affirming our oneness with the Creator and all creation.

As we live and walk and breathe and sing our songs and tell our stories, so are we cocreating history, coauthoring a new mythology that will free us all from bondage to bad ideas. We are writers of the new sacred texts, scribes of a new story of the cosmos and our intimate roll in its unfolding. We are mirrors to one another's mission and meaning, for ultimately we have all come here to light up the world. It is through our consciousness that the planet is seeing itself, evolving itself, turning waves of Supreme Intelligence into particles of information.

To merge with this reality is to know bliss. To understand our lives as the immediate apprehension of supreme reality is to be in nirvana. To comprehend yourself as a perfect thought of the Creator, a word made flesh, is to plant your feet firmly on the spiritual path.

One Way

Christian churches made a terrible mistake when they announced that theirs was the one true faith. It was a quantum leap backward for Christianity to proclaim that salvation can be found only through Jesus Christ. There is nothing redeeming, prophetic, compassionate, or even "Christian" about this statement.

Consider the Eskimo who asked the priest, "'If I did not know about God and sin, would I go to hell?"

The priest says, "No, not if you did not know."

The Eskimo says, "Then why did you tell me?"

There could never *be* one true faith, for faith is most essentially the *living out* of our commitments and ultimate concerns. We identify for ourselves those ultimate issues, based on our understanding of the world and our role in it. This is how we shape and develop our spirituality. It is how we evolve ourselves, how we move forward on the path. We keep defining and redefining our relationship with the cosmos, the earth, the Creator, and all of creation. We notice what breaks our hearts, where we are needed. We see what is broken and we resolve to fix it. We listen to our body's wisdom and discern constantly where we are being called. And the answer is always connected to our heart's desire. Joy is the compass point for this discernment. If you could solve any global problem in the world, which one would bring you the most joy to solve?

Your answer to that is a clue to your next step on the spiritual path. We must move in the direction of our joy. It is not selfish to do that, not egotistical, not self-serving. It is enlightened and inspired. Ramana Maharshi, the Indian mystic, said: "Your own self-realization is the greatest service you can render the world." The direction in which your heart calls you is the only right way for you to move. Others may criticize you, blame you, be angry with you for not being there for their needs, but your job is to stay true to the call of *your* heart. It may feel countercultural, or even counterintuitive for a while if you have been a victim of others' bad ideas all your life, but if you have come this far on your path, it is time to go the whole way and be true to your soul's mission. If that's troublesome, remember the words of the Jesuit retreat director Tony de Mello: "Do what you want. That's not selfish. Selfish is expecting *other* people to do what you want."

This has nothing to do with creeds and beliefs. There is nothing to defend or learn or repeat to others. Your spirituality is your own private plan for action. It is the blueprint for your life, your internal GPS. It guides you to right action. To be a spiritual person, you need not have a set of beliefs to which you subscribe. You *may* have, but your spirituality is not contingent on that. It is not what you believe, but how you act that matters, as in "they will know you by your fruits." A person who watched you in action for one week would conclude that you were committed to something and would say, "That person cares about this or that." That's what your integrity is about. That's how you live an authentic life—you make sure that what you do is in alignment with what you are committed to and what you believe is important.

This afternoon a woman knocked on my door, and when I peeked my head out she asked, "Hi there. I have a question. What do you think is the most terrible problem in the world today?" That was an interesting approach for a missionary, I thought, but I decided to engage.

"I think it's a twofold problem," I said. "One is that religions are becoming more intolerant of diversity, and two, that they keep encouraging people to think of God as some faraway, personified being instead of the very Energy within and all around them."

"Good" she says. "So you believe in God."

"Only the one inside me," I said.

"Good!" she said, not taking me in for a second.

"And since you believe in our great God Jehovah, I assume you know how important it is what we call Him. Our name for Him is very important."

"I don't think of God as a person with a sex."

"Yes, good, and you know that Jehovah has given us a book that explains in detail what we need to do to get to Him."

"Yes, I know about that book, which was written for those times, 2500 years ago. I think we're here to write new sacred texts. Prophets didn't live only in biblical times. These times are calling for *us* to be prophetic, don't you think?"

"Jehovah has told us in detail . . ." she continued, as if my words had turned to dust before they entered her eardrums. Just then the phone rang.

"So sorry, I have to go," I said, and she pulled a pamphlet out of her purse and handed it to me before she left.

Loving intolerance. She was most kind but would not take in the possibility that my way was a valid way on the path to enlightenment. We could have been there all day, but there was no opening for dialogue. She was there to save me. I am here to say we do not need saving, except from our fear and ignorance and any notion that there is only one way to go on the spiritual path.

Many things feel blasphemous to us when we are first starting out on our individual path. Something feels terribly wrong about thinking of ourselves as prophets, when we are still in the grip of traditional religion. Thinking of our own selves as sacred, as vessels of the Divine, or even the hands and eyes and ears of the Creator—it feels frightening to some to allow for that possibility, to reframe our image of God in those terms. But it is only our religious brainwashing that causes that. Native Americans don't feel that way. Hindus and Buddhists don't feel that way. Tribal people around the world do not feel that way. It is western Christianity that has an investment in the faraway, transcendent male deity that we have all learned about from childhood.

But this religion has not supported our spiritual evolution. It has not taught us how to deepen our spirituality, to transform our relationship with the Source from parent-child to cocreators. It has perpetuated creeds and dogmas that have kept us infantilized, caused us to abdicate our power as cocreators of this culture and civilization. It has kept us from being compassionate at times, referring to God as some Geppetto in the sky, pulling strings for his own secret reasons. Ask anyone who is grieving the loss of a loved one how it feels to have God mentioned as a reason not to be sad.

To be on a spiritual path does not mean that you turn your back on all the gifts that our religions have given to us. No— the opposite is true. You review your relationship with religion with great care. You discern what is valuable, loving, and true for you, and you discard what insults your soul. Then you will be pushed by the wisdom of the past and pulled by the call and demands of the future. As Albert Einstein writes, "The religion of the future will be a cosmic religion. It will have to transcend a personal God and avoid dogma and theology. Encompassing both the natural and the spiritual, it will have to be based on a religious sense arising from the experience of all things, natural and spiritual, considered as a meaningful unity."

You will see then that there are prophets and mystics in these times who are moving us forward, just as the prophets and mystics of old did in their time. And how do you know them? By their actions, just as others know *you* by your actions.

In his book *With Open Hands,* Henri Nouwen, the Dutch-born priest and author, writes that prophets are people who attract others by their inner power. "Those who meet them are fascinated by them and want to know more about them. All who come in contact with them get the irresistible impression that they derive their strength from a hidden source which is strong and rich. An inner freedom flows out from them, giving them an independence which is neither haughty nor aloof, but which enables them to stand above immediate needs and the most pressing necessities."

When you find your right way, your path of spiritual practice and joyful action, then you will acquire this inner power. You will act from the truest authority—your own. And those who know you will know, too, that the source of your light is infinite and ever flowing, as it is the Source of All Light that moves you.

Chapter Eleven

Crossroad

The writer Nancy Mairs once wrote that "whenever one speaks of God, God goes stiff as a corpse." I caution people against using the word *God* in my workshops, encouraging them to come up with a phrase that says what they want to say without using that word. It's a spiritual exercise, and people often balk, wanting to resort to the old, easy catch-phrase. But the trouble is twofold: one, you never know what the term means for the person you are with; and two, when you bring up God, people's attention and focus often leaves the immediate, local situation and travels heavenward to who knows where. It's like letting the air out of the balloon of human possibility. If you say, "Don't worry. It's all in God's hands," you are abdicating your authority to a certain extent, saying that someone else will take care of business.

I am not denying that there may be some higher power at work, some cocreative force that we are in consort with, but *this* world, *these* crises, *these* choices before us are in *our* hands. The cosmos is being created by the mind of the Infinite One, but the world we live in is being created by the minds of the finite ones—by us.

Those of us who are consciously evolving ourselves, who are cocreating—to the best of our ability—a culture and civilization that we can be proud of, are mindful of the power of language. We are undoing for ourselves, and helping our fellow humans undo, the damage that religious concepts and language have caused over the millennia.

We are at a point in history in which "humans have to choose between adoration and suicide," writes Teilhard de Chardin. The adoration of which he speaks is an earthy, biological, reverential understanding of our complete oneness with the earth, from which we rose, and the heavens, which we contain. Ninety-three percent of the mass in our bodies is stardust. We are made of billions of atoms that are actually hydrogen dust remnants from the big bang. What would be more appropriate than feeling adoration for the cosmos that birthed us and sustains us?

If we had been influenced by a cosmology of reverence, a mythology of wonder and awe over all these centuries, we would not be facing the environmental crises we are facing today. We would not have torn apart science and religion, male and female, Christian and Jew, black and white. We would not have created a world of dualism and competition, greed and warfare. We would not have a world where half the people are dieting and half are starving.

A culture or civilization cannot lift itself out of a deadening and destructive mindset, but creative ideas and actions from a few can reignite the moral imagination of the many. And we are those few. We are the ones taking our spirituality into our own hands. We are the ones creating new stories, new language, new images of a world that can work for everyone. Paul Hawken's book *Blessed Unrest* offers a description of humanity's collective genius and our unstoppable movement to reimagine our relationship with the environment and with one another. This movement that we're engaged in has no name, leader, or location. It is ignored by the media. But, like nature itself, it is organizing from the grassroots up, in every city, town, and culture, and is emerging to be an extraordinary expression of our human need to be of use, to do good, to live our faith.

Our creativity is our faith in running shoes. The stories we tell, the pictures we share, the words we write, the poems we compose—all these are outgrowths of what we believe is important, that to which we are committed. Our spirituality comes to life in our actions, our relationships, and our creations. It is about what we *do*, not what we think. And more importantly, it is about what we do *together,* for this evolutionary act that we are engaged in is a cocreative experiment.

Philosopher Jacob Needleman suggests that group pondering is the art form of the future. In our groups, we are collective conduits for spiritual intelligence to localize and materialize. As we circle, share silence, open ourselves to the Infinite, and reveal ourselves to one another, we practice the art of group pondering. We dare to ask the question and look straight into the deep unknown. The past does not interest us. The present is our ground and the future pulls us toward it.

As we lean into it, learn to risk, learn to let go, then we open ourselves to the new words from the cosmos. We hear the new language, see the new pathways, find the right metaphors to share the revelations as they unfold. As we learn to hear one another into being, we witness the miracle of ongoing creation. We see the universe expanding through our thoughts and our increasing complexity. We watch ourselves think beyond duality and act beyond self-interest, knowing that our well-being is tied to the well-being of all.

"'Spiritual' is not necessarily [about] religion," writes Jacob Needleman. "A spiritual impulse draws a person toward inner meaning, toward the intangible, toward the enhancement of consciousness and the search to serve the dignity of mankind." Many thousands of us are at a crossroads right now; we are leaving our churches to find the Divine who dwells inside us, who propels our actions from within, who is the breath that breathes us, the voice that leads us. We do not have answers to offer up, but our questions are common and deep and magnetic, drawing toward them the groups that will ponder and pause.

Communities are rising up around the world in response to our questions, and it is these communities that will lead us past our illusions, beyond our fears, and into a reality brighter and bolder than any of our imaginings. We are attendants at the wake of the old way, midwifing a new world into existence. This is our destiny and our purpose, and when we wake up to this tremendous privilege, when we sense the oak in the acorn of our selves, then we will move mountains and shift the tides. Or as the great mystic Teilhard de Chardin says, "Someday after mastering winds, waves, tides and gravity, we shall harness the energies of love. And then, for the second time in the history of the world, man will discover fire."

An Apostle's Creed

I believe that the Source of Creation is an Incomprehensible Mystery radiating through the cosmos as Supreme Intelligence, Absolute Love, Ineffable Beauty.

I believe that human beings are carriers of cosmic consciousness and agents of its evolution.

I believe that the Source from which we come is alive in us as our breath, and as we speak and sing and breathe, we release the beauty of the Creator into the world.

I believe that the universe is unfolding through me, and that it is through my being that it is becoming self-aware.

I believe that Nature—our Mother—has the answer to all our questions.

I believe that it is through our consciousness that creation and all its multiplicity is knowing itself, evolving itself, and converging into its original Oneness.

I believe that the greatest challenge for humans is to free ourselves from religious trappings and cultural constraints that perpetuate our powerlessness and dependence on external forces.

I believe that the bliss we are seeking erupts spontaneously when we are faithful to our soul's mission.

I believe that healing the wounds of the earth and its people is a holy act that, in itself, heals us.

I believe that our worldviews create the world we experience, and as we alter them, we alter our lives and the world entire.

Book Club Guidelines

1. **Stop.** Each of you share a consciousness-raising experience that seriously changed your life. What did it cause you to stop doing? The author talks about the importance of balance in our lives. What strategies do you have in place to help you stay balanced? Do you engage in regular activities that feed these aspects of yourself: emotional, mental, physical, spiritual?

2. **Lane Ends.** The author writes that our faith is tied to our ultimate commitments and concerns as we experience them in the living of our lives. Spend some time sharing with one another about the things you feel committed to. You have had a lot of beliefs handed down to you that you may or may not still believe in. Mention one or two things that you believe to be true based on your experience of being alive.

3. **Yield.** Do certain events in your life seem to keep you from being happy somehow? Do you have a feeling that someone else is responsible for your joy? Whom do you tend to blame when things go wrong? What might happen if you took personal responsibility for the way things work out? Can you think of a time in your life when you surrendered or let go of your need to control? Take some time to share these stories.

4. **Curves Ahead.** What does it mean to you to be in awe? In your speaking, do you find that you often refer to God?

Reflect back to Susan Griffin's poem, that we are "nature seeing nature / . . . / Nature weeping. / Nature speaking of nature to nature." How does this make you feel? How do you feel when you are in nature? What is your favorite place to go and why?

5. **Divided Highway.** Walt Whitman writes about reexamining all we have been told and dismissing "whatever insults your soul." What does that statement mean to you? Share some stories about ideas, actions, and beliefs that you were taught to maintain but have since let go. What did they tell you about being a girl or a boy, a wife or a husband? What did they tell you about your religion? About other religions? About other cultural groups and/ or races?

6. **End Divided Highway.** The doctors the author wrote of kept their spirituality locked up inside them. Do you tend to do that? When do you feel safe enough to share about your spiritual life? The author also wrote about

holding two opposing thoughts in your mind at the same time. Do you notice yourself doing that? Can you hear an opposing idea without feeling you have to defend your own? If you were going to have lunch with a person you feel is your "enemy" or "the other," think of a few questions you would ask that person.

7. **Falling Rocks Ahead.** How might you respond to believers who think you should believe a certain way to "be saved?" If you left your church, what parts do you think you would miss most? Thousands of people around the country are participating in "house church" on Sunday mornings. It's taking all kinds of forms, and it's very creative and communal. If you were to plan a ritual for a group of people who have left their churches but still want to be part of a spiritual community, what might the ritual look like?

8. **Men at Work.** Does Deepak Chopra's statement that "effort is the problem, not the solution" ring true for you?

Share your response to Meister Eckhart's statement that enlightenment is a process of subtraction, not addition. What do you do to increase your personal awareness? Do you have an "ugly American" story like the author's story about being in India? What did you learn from it? How conscious are you of all the words that come out of your mouth? How can you increase such awareness?

9. **Merge.** Tell a story about a time when someone was really present to you and what a difference that made in your life. Have you ever been present like that to another person? Do you consider yourself a good talking partner? Can you refrain from offering your opinion? How do you understand the assertion that "you create your own circumstances"? Is this true for you?

10. **One Way.** Talk about how your spirituality has changed over the years. How are you living out your commitments? If you had a magic wand and could heal any global wound, what would you fix? What breaks your

heart the most? If someone were to watch you closely for one week, what might that person think you value? What does it mean to be a modern-day prophet? Could you ever be one?

11. **Crossroads.** What brings you the most hope these days? Jacob Needleman writes about group pondering being the art form of our times. You have been engaged in group pondering as you've discussed these questions and your responses to this book. How has group pondering affected your life? Does it feel intimate? Frightening? Consciousness-raising?

How do you describe the distinction between spiritual and religious? How can leaving religion behind deepen your own spirituality?

Further Readings

Anderson, Sarah, ed. *Heaven's Face Thinly Veiled: A Book of Spiritual Writing by Women*. Boston: Shambhala, 1998.

Bergson, Henri. *Creative Evolution*. Mineola, New York: Dover Publications, 1998.

Berry, Thomas. *The Christian Future and the Fate of Earth*. Edited by Mary Evelyn Tucker and John Grim. New York: Orbis Books, 2009.

———. *The Sacred Universe: Earth, Spirituality, and Religion in the Twenty-First Century*. New York: Columbia University Press, 2009.

Borg, Marcus. *Meeting Jesus Again for the First Time: The Historical Jesus and the Heart of Contemporary Faith*. New York: HarperCollins, 1994.

Bruteau, Beatrice. *God's Ecstasy: The Creation of a Self-Creating World*. New York: Crossroad Publishing, 1997.

———. *Radical Optimism: Practical Spirituality in an Uncertain World*. Boulder, CO: Sentient Publications, 2002.

De Chardin, Pierre Teilhard. *Divine Milieu*. New York: Harper & Row, 1960.

———. *The Heart of Matter*. Orlando, FL: Harcourt & Brace, 1976.

———. *The Phenomenon of Man*. New York: Harper & Row, 1955.

Eckhart, Meister. *Meister Eckhart: Selections from His Essential Writings*. Edited by Emilie Griffin. Translated by

Edmund Colledge and Bernard McGinn. San Francisco: HarperSanFrancisco, 2005.

Eisler, Riane. *The Chalice and the Blade: Our History, Our Future*. San Francisco, HarperSanFrancisco, 1995.

———. *Sacred Pleasure: Sex, Myth, and the Politics of the Body—New Paths to Power and Love*. San Francisco: HarperSanFrancisco, 1995.

Hafiz. *The Gift: Poems by Hafiz, the Great Sufi Master*. Translated by Daniel Ladinsky. New York: Penguin Arkana, 1999.

Hirschfield, Jane, ed. *Women in Praise of the Sacred: 43 Centuries of Spiritual Poetry by Women*. New York: HarperCollins, 1994.

Hubbard, Barbara Marx. *Birth 2012 and Beyond: Humanity's Great Shift to the Age of Conscious Evolution*. San Francisco, CA: Shift Books, 2012.

———. *Conscious Evolution: Awakening Our Social Potential*. Novato, CA: New World Library, 1998.

Ladinsky, Daniel. *Love Poems from God: Twelve Sacred Voices from the East and West*. New York: Penguin Company, 2002.

Lipton, Bruce. *The Biology of Belief*. Santa Rosa, CA: Mountain of Love Books, 2005.

McTaggart, Lynne. *The Bond: How to Fix Your Falling-Down World*. New York: Free Press, 2011.

Mindell, Arnold. *Quantum Mind: The Edge Between Physics and Psychology*. Portland, OR: Lao Tse Press, 2000.

O'Murchu, Diarmuid. *Ancestral Grace: Meeting God in Our Human Story*. New York: Orbis Books, 2008.

———. *Evolutionary Faith*. New York: Orbis Books, 1970.

———. *Quantum Theology: Spiritual Implications of the New Physics*. New York: Crossroad Publishing, 1998.

Pearce, Joseph Chilton. *The Biology of Transcendence: A Blueprint of the Human Spirit*. Rochester, VT: Park Street Press, 2002.

———. *The Heart-Mind Matrix: How the Heart Can Teach*

the Mind New Ways to Think. Rochester, VT: Park Street Press, 2010.

———. *Spiritual Initiation and the Breakthrough of Consciousness: The Bond of Power*. Rochester, VT: *Inner Traditions*, 2003.

Pearsall, Paul. *The Heart's Code: Tapping the Wisdom and Power of Our Heart Energy*. New York: Broadway Books, 1998.

Phillips, Jan. *The Art of Original Thinking: The Making of a Thought Leader*. San Diego, CA: 9th Element Press, 2006.

———. *No Ordinary Time: The Rise of Spiritual Intelligence and Evolutionary Creativity*. San Diego, CA: Livingkindness Foundation, 2011.

Pink, Daniel H. *Drive: The Surprising Truth About What Motivates Us*. New York: Riverhead Books, 2009.

———. *A Whole New Mind: Why Right-Brainers Will Rule the Future*. New York: Riverhead Books, 2006.

Spong, John Shelby. *Jesus for the Non-Religious*. San Francisco: HarperCollins, 2007.

———. *A New Christianity for a New World: Why Traditional Faith Is Dying and How a New Faith Is Being Born.* New York: HarperCollins, 2001.

———. *Rescuing the Bible from Fundamentalism: A Bishop Rethinks the Meaning of Scripture.* New York: HarperCollins, 1991.

Swimme, Brian. *The Hidden Heart of the Cosmos: Humanity and the New Story.* New York: Orbis Books, 1996.

Underhill, Evelyn. *Mysticism: The Nature and Development of Spiritual Consciousness.* Oxford: Oneworld Publications, 1999.

Quest Books

encourages open-minded inquiry into
world religions, philosophy, science, and the arts
in order to understand the wisdom of the ages,
respect the unity of all life, and help people explore
individual spiritual self-transformation.

Its publications are generously supported by
The Kern Foundation,
a trust committed to Theosophical education.

Quest Books is the imprint of
the Theosophical Publishing House,
a division of the Theosophical Society in America.
For information about programs, literature,
on-line study, membership benefits, and international centers,
see www.theosophical.org
or call 800-669-1571 or (outside the U.S.) 630-668-1571.

Related Quest Titles

To order books or a complete Quest catalog,
call 800-669-9425 or (outside the U.S.) 630-665-0130.

Jan Phillips is an internationally known author and speaker. Her workshops have been sponsored by the International Women's Writing Guild, and her award-winning photographs and articles appear in the *New York Times*, *Christian Science Monitor*, *Utne Reader*, and other national publications. She has presented at the National Organization for Women and dozens of universities and spent three years as a contributing artist and coeditor of the annual Women Artists Datebook. Her books include *The Art of Original Thinking: The Making of a Thought Leader*, *God Is at Eye Level: Photography as a Healing Art*, and the award-winning *Marry Your Muse: Making a Lasting Commitment to Your Creativity*. See www.janphillips.com.